CARSON WOLFE

# BOY(ISH)
# VEST

Published in 2022
Hidden Voice Publishing
www.hiddenvoicepublishing.co.uk

Cover Art By: Maxine Harlow

For my wife Fae
& our three children,
May, Keiana & Sojourner

These poems are a curation of my best published works from 2020-2022, including new, never-before-seen poems.

# CONTENTS

## BOY(ISH) VEST

# BOY(ISH) VEST

## BUDAPEST

The waitress is ignoring me on purpose.
In this foreign restaurant, my queerness
translates in the barber's blade,

the offspring of new hickeys
assaulting the waitress with teeth marks
trailing down my collar bone, leading to—

unwelcome thoughts of how they got there.
I strayed three blocks from the haven
of the party hostel, clothes still damp

from my fumble in communal showers
with a bisexual Canadian. BOY(ISH)
written in bold on my vest, a word

I wear quietly here
like *excuse me*, and *please*.

She brings the bill on demand
to the family who have eaten
three courses. For the third time,

I tell her I am ready to order.
I am still here, waiting
until my clothes have dried

and set like rigor mortis
in the shape of my wishful thinking.
This booth, the final resting place

to my benefit of the doubt. The knife
and fork placed on a black serviette
are flowers on a casket spelling out

my loss, filling my empty stomach
with a banquet of air.

# THE TSA AGENT DIVIDES MY FAMILY BY RACE

Regular families pass through, whole.
I am ordered to step back with the white child
who looks most like me.          My wife waved forward
            with the black child who looks most like her.

I think, ok, this is America,
at least they got to go first.

*It could be worse* is a mindset
which makes no big deal

about us being split
like a pie chart in equal halves.

A statistic of queer families
who move through this world

as *just friends,* or single moms
who met in a support group

returning from a field trip
to Frida Kahlo's Casa Azul.

She is snatched through security,
fast-tracking the possibility

that we're not invisible at all,
that my plaid shirt has turned

the airport into a pride parade.
That her sunflower dress

means she can still be saved.
I can see them, beyond

a glass wall, scanning the crowd

for faces which complete

the smiling photo on our mantel.
I can hear our daughter's voice

answering, *this is my mum,*
*yes, I'm sure, this is my mum.*

# CHOOSE YOUR OWN ADVENTURE

You wake in a decade you are too young to know, dating a guy ten years older than you. The smell of bacon wafts from the stove where you imagine him cooking you breakfast in bed. He has arranged the serving tray with care, a blunt knife, a lump of soft butter, a fresh garden flower in your grandmother's vase. You count the petals, predict the odds are in your favour for a game of *he loves me, he loves me not.* The singed fat thickens the air, settling into your hair, oiled and wet like an abattoir. You are vegetarian. Your home distorts into the Hacienda, he is playing music you never danced to, because you were busy playing dress-up in your mother's shoes, preparing to fill them with boyfriends who throw your heirloom ornaments at the wall. The DVD shelf is loaded with classic gangster movies, and you can now pick Ray Liotta out of a lineup, but you can't pick up the phone when your friends call. The fridge is crayoned with art from the previous child he is only allowed supervised contact with. This is none of your business. The sofa bought on credit is stained with a domestic turned 999. It faces an empty rectangle of dust where the TV once distracted your daughter before he stole it. The table is a grave scattered with a bouquet of used alcohol wipes. Your lip is a coffin lid, mauled from the inside like fingernail scratches from a girl buried alive. You investigate in the bathroom mirror, find his name tattooed backwards in your mouth. Each nostril is blocked with begging the dealer to return at 4am. Your throat is closing now too. You claw at yourself, a rat, going for your own neck. What do you do next?

1.  Patchwork the hoard of red flags into an apron, cook a steak dinner, serve it bleeding. Everything appears normal. Turn to page 19.

2.  After fighting all night over another man you definitely did *not* look at, wake back up in a decade you are too young to know. Repeat for at least eight months.

3. Burn his passport and head to the airport with the last of your dole money. When an agent official asks how much you are travelling with, lie like the expert you have become. Turn to page 18.

# IN-FLIGHT ANNOUNCEMENT

Welcome onboard this service from a fixed address
to elective homelessness. On behalf of the crew,
I ask that you do not approach our survival briefing
with the attitude of 'it will never happen to me'.
When the captain turns, warning signals may alert you
to fasten in for turbulence. Signals appear red,
behind a compliment, or not at all.
In the event of a break-in, stay calm and assume
the mama-bear position (grab the sturdiest wooden toy,
brace for impact). Should the cabin experience sudden panic,
a blood-knuckled hand will drop down from above.
Place it over your mouth to smother a scream.
Pull the thumb to release the security deposit to a fist
shaped hole in the wall. If you are travelling with children,
I'm sorry.

When evacuating, follow the hysteria of alarms
installed by child services that triggered
each time your daughter placed palms to pane.
Exits are not clearly marked. Exits are lit with family photos.
Exits lead to a hallway where no neighbours come to assist.
Stow away your left arm, use this time to think of a new story
for when passengers ask, *who tattooed your sleeve?*
The temperature at our destination is hot enough to kill
any blame still leeching on your skin. If you forgot
to pack sunscreen, we offer a nontoxic
solution that blocks all harmful light – including gaslight.
For your safety, we have replaced all life-vests
with celibacy rings disguised as mosquito repellent.
As we prepare for take-off, make an erasure poem
from the police report you carry in your purse
like the photo of a loved one.
Thank you for choosing to fill a bag not shaped
like your body. We wish you safe passage,
and a tag tied to your luggage, not your big toe.

# THEY'LL SAY HE WAS A QUIET BOY, VERY ODD

My boyfriend skins a rabbit. Butchers
midway to the flank, before he throws it
half-dressed with fur, into the neighbour's
recycling bin.

He always does half a job. Ties intricate knots
in the garbage bag, but never takes it out.
Unrolls the notes, but leaves an outline of chalk
on my daughter's princess mirror.

My boyfriend skins a rabbit, but it's only a hobby,
a Ray Mears copycat—the bushcraft loner,
not the other show-off who drinks his own piss
for a hydrated camera crew.

My boyfriend's weapon collection is growing
with my will for him to stop bringing home gifts
that make my doorstep stink. He thinks himself
a modern-day Thoreau, lawless in the woods.

My boyfriend trails a scent of Dahmer's childhood.
When my daughter asks for a kitten,
I pretend I have allergies. When he isn't looking,
I check lamp-posts for missing posters.

When my boyfriend sneaks out at night, he whittles
my sense of self with the precision of a survivalist,
and I'm certain he would be first in the apocalypse
to eat the friend who is slowest to run.

My boyfriend brings home a gun, says it's for hunting,
and I don't ask why he keeps putting it in my hands,
why he crowds me like a girl with a snooker cue
and no clue how to aim. Why he focuses my shot

on the two lovebirds outside my window.
Why I behave as if the silencer is screwed

into my own jaw. I just shoot feathers
from the branch, with one pull of the trigger.

And he lifts me from behind, cheering,
as if I potted the black in the darkest corner
of his heart, as if this is the proudest
he has ever been.

# ALRIGHT NOW, LADS, WHICH ONE OF YOU IS IT?

*The Police launched a public manhunt for The Yorkshire Ripper. A tape of his voice was broadcast several times a day on television and radio stations. One million pounds were spent on billboards plastered all over Britain asking DO YOU RECOGNISE HIS HANDWRITING? - Esquire*

All the coppers got, were wives
convinced their husbands

had once written love notes
in the same scrawl.

The phone lines would not stop
him from killing again.

Still, there were hundreds of officers
numb from the deadweight

of the receivers. In the first week,
twenty thousand women

called to report, without a doubt,
their boyfriend was *The Ripper.*

There were filing cabinets so heavy
with the names of English men.

Engineers had to install concrete pillars
to hold the floor from caving in.

# TED BUNDY GROUPIE PREPARES FOR HIS TRIAL

In the hair colour aisle, I search for his favourite shade,
bark under nail brown, bottom of the lake brown,
one closest to his mother's brown. Stain the motel sheets

with dreams of how I've been preparing for him
in the arms of fishermen that know the trophy weight
equivalent to a dead girl. The papers say I am lovesick,

sick for love—sick, but I won't give them the satisfaction
of an absent father. I give them hair parted down the middle,
silver hoops in place of debutante studs, weighted

in solidarity with the cuffs dragging between his ankles.
Broadcasters will ask, *why are you here?* I'll stand in a lineup
of women and say, I have always been a dead girl

walking. Alone, in the city at night, never using my house key
as *just* a house key. I want him to look at me, to feel blue
eyes imagining another life being drained.

I want to turn this court pew into a church, become a bride
in black marching down death row, screaming *I do I do*.
Because if I can survive him, I can survive anything.

# FREE LOVE AT TAMERA

*Love is a state of being that can't be possessed or regulated by laws* - Tamera.org

I bet my tour guide hosts somatic orgies
when outsiders like me aren't visiting.
In the community garden, he is a god
plucking acidic grapes from a vine,
testing for ripeness. The village is as quiet
as a white woman on a silent retreat.
Everyone must be inside their eco-huts
shagging. A nudist free-for-all. Maybe
It's more civilised than I think. Maybe
I'm not European enough for this. Maybe
when the guidelines say *authentic consent matters,*
It means that upon residence, each girl
must be tested on her ability to say no.
I'd be required to show I've never accepted
a piece of cake I didn't like just because
it was bought for me. Or drank from the red sea
parting my mind

from my body,
just because it was uncorked for me.
That I've never passed out at a party,
woke to breath fogging the hourglass
of my thighs and pretended
to be asleep.

# DO YOU FEEL PERSONALLY ATTACKED CHRIS BROWN IS STILL MAKING MUSIC?

yes | no

kill the radio / run
fast / from society
i promise your body can / breathe and
heal from the bruises / unlearn the violence of
boys will be / boys hold them
accountable / at a fist's length
for their behaviour / unfollow Rhianna
smash cds in hmv / destroy
whilst singing *i love* / the way you lie
*with freedom* / to convince yourself
it was never your fault / control is yours

## DICK GHAZAL

Me to my girlfriend: I got you a gift, it's my dick
in a box. Jokes on you Justin Timberlake, my dick
came in a box, it cost an arm and a leg—a third leg.
I put a condom on for realism, my dick
is protected! Then she moans cum inside me
and I pull out like Mae Martin, who strapped a dick
on Netflix, inspired me to write a poem
about being semi-boy and wearing a dick
labelled sex toy. But this is no game, I assure,
as it glows in the dark, aurora borealis dick,
spread across celestial sheets asking why?
why was I born without a dick?

# IN RESPONSE TO THE EMISSIONS OF BABY MAKING

Our sperm donor gifted us energy saving light bulbs, which isn't as weird as it sounds when you understand we gifted him organic granola first. He saved us fifty quid on leccy that year, a dent in the emissions of our baby making. It took five thousand miles and a hunk of plastic ovulation tests for my wife and I to birth a child into this world. I don't know if it's my daughter's coo warming my heart, or her tiny footprints tarnished with carbon before she exhaled dioxide for the first time. We tell ourselves the worst action against overpopulation is sitting back and letting the Tories breed. At least we haven't used tampons since 2013. Capitalists pollute and poison then point at me to justify her life with a biodegradable baby wipe. I'm pointing at the blackberries that bloom in the wrong season. My daughter is pointing at a picture of a bee, and I'm hoping she will be stung by one.

# AN EPISODE OF PLANET EARTH ON THE DYING HABITAT OF DYKE BARS

A Butch-Femme couple, silvered with age,
enter a woodland the neighbouring airport
plans to flatten with concrete.

In the winter of their lives,
I want to lend them my summer,
offer the liquorice tea in my flask,

ask if they teach gender studies,
if they met at Moody Gardens,
or some other lesbian bar

before they were bulldozed
by the corporate tornado
that bypassed bars for men.

I need to know if they U-Hauled
on the first date or the second,
if they still fuck like secret teens.

I want to archive their herstory,
carve all three of our clits
into wet cement. Holy trinity,

holy elders, holy cunts of permanence.
I want to tattoo dyke on my fist.
To be more than a person

passing queer family on a hike,
who only nods to say, *I see you,*
then continues, onwards,

alone.

# TEN WEEKS

The contractions start in a coastal cafe. You push
scrambled tofu around your plate, it's too late

for sanitary towels so I line the car seat with a *bag for life*
to drive you, curled and panting to our bathtub.

I peel the leggings from your thighs, and stare
at the eagle tattoo, its permanence. I hold out hands

to catch our belly-up fish, but miss. Our little gem,
prized from shell. I scoop it up, like a child, a child.

*You finally have one up on my exes,* I joke. *I've held a few hearts*
*but never a placenta.* And just like that, we are laughing

aboard our shipwrecked family. *We'll have a thousand babies,*
I promise, as you peek into my palms

and marvel at our treasure.

# ACKNOWLEDGEMENTS

Thank you to my first reader, Fae. None of this would be possible without you.

Thank you to Lexi Pelle for editing these poems. I trust you completely with all my words.

Thank you to Megan Falley, Melissa Sussens, Nikki Allen, and the rest of our Poems That Don't Suck writing community, you are the anchors to my clouds.

Thank you to Joanna for proofreading.

Thank you to Button for selecting *Ten Weeks* as a category winner of the 2021 Video Contest.

Thank you to Ergon Theatre for choosing *In Response to the Emissions of Baby Making* to be part of the Get Heard Project. Thank you also to Contact Theatre for providing studio space and Reform Radio for broadcasting.

Thank you to Fourteen Poems for including *An Episode of Planet Earth on the Dying Habitat of Dyke Bars* in issue five of the print anthology, and thank you to Writing East Midlands for selecting it as an Aurora Prize Winner for 2021.

Thank you to the following journals where versions of these poems first appeared:

Freezeray Poetry – *Dick Ghazal* & *Do you feel personally attacked chris brown is still making music?*

Ghost City Review – *Free Love at Tamera*

Quail Bell Magazine – *The TSA Agent Divides my Family by Race*

The Penn Review – *Choose Your Own Adventure, In-flight Announcement* & *They'll say he was a quiet boy, very odd*

Thank you to Sarah Pritchard and Joel Sadler-Puckering for giving my poems this space to live together on the page.

Thank you to everyone who chooses to spend a moment of their wild and beautiful lives reading my words, what an honour.

NOTES

The title, alright now, lads, which one of you is it? was taken from the subheading of an article covering The Yorkshire Ripper case published by esquire in 1981.

Ted Bundy groupie prepares for his trial was inspired by Sierra DeMulder's poem Mrs Dahmer.

Moody Gardens was a lesbian bar running in Lowell Massachusetts from 1957 until being forced to close in 1964.

REVEIWS OF BOY(ISH) VEST

In their unflinching and uncompromising truth-telling, Boy(ish) Vest's deeply personal and compelling poems challenge the reader to not look away from the everyday horrors of misogyny, male violence, queer invisibility, and economic inequality. Yet, through Carson Wolfe's authentic writing and fresh imagery, there is real hope here too. Wolfe wants us to see the personal exit ramp from these horrors: love, family, solidarity, owning your queerness in whatever form it takes. An exciting debut that shows Wolfe as an impassioned poet already aware of their own voice and willing to use it to shine a light on the broken elements of society (and urge us to join them in fixing these elements). As they write: "I can survive anything". These poems are a call to arms for us all.

— Ben Townley-Canning, Fourteen Poems


Through innovative use of form, Wolfe illuminates not just violence, but our complicity with it, in all its forms. These poems somehow balance anger with love, despair with hope to create an unforgettable, wild, risk-taking roller-coaster of a book.

— Dr Kim Moore, author of 'What the Trumpet Taught Me' (Smith | Doorstop, 2022) and 'All the Men I Never Married' (Seren, 2021)


An excellent collection of adventure and thought. To process and capture moments in everyday life as elaborate as Wolfe does with their life is like looking through a picture book.

— Shanel Morae, Spoken Word Artist & author of My Words

In Boy(ish) Vest, Carson Wolfe expertly weaves us into their world with a voice that feels both intimate and urgent, both comforting and unrelentingly bare. These poems are a meditation on "choosing to fill a bag not shaped / like your body", on dreams for the next generation to have a "childhood / with grass stains and mud pies" and on knowing what it means "to get comfortable / in arms that know the trophy weight /equivalent to a dead girl". Wolfe writes as if to write is to breathe, as if putting these stories to the page is an act of more than survival, but of thriving too. Boy(ish) Vest will leave you awed by Carson's use of form and line breaks, moved by their masterful artistry with imagery, and awed by their ability to create beauty from the pain that is existing in this world as a queer person, as a survivor of domestic violence, as a parent. I was devoured by these poems in the best way.

— Melissa Sussens, author of Slaughterhouse (Karavan Press, 2022)


Carson Wolfe's poems pulse with the heat and electricity of claiming stake to a body born for authentically living, loving, and breaking the mold. A lyrically sharp collection that sings with defiance and humor before bringing you to your knees with the tenderness of vulnerability. Boy(ish) Vest is a stunning read that 'nods to say, I see you.'

— Sheleen McElhinney, author of Every Little Vanishing (Write Bloody Publishing, 2022)

# HIDDEN VOICE PUBLISHING

Hidden Voice Publishing is an independent publishing resource centre that supports & represents authors from under-represented groups with publishing paperback and Amazon Kindle books.

# TITLES ON HIDDEN VOICE PUBLISHING

*I KNOW WHY THE GAY MAN DANCES*
*JOEL SADLER-PUCKERING*

*INKY BLACK WOMAN*
*MINA AIDOO*

*FERAL ANIMALS*
*JOEL SADLER-PUCKERING*

*WHEN WOMEN FLY*
*SARAH PRITCHARD*

*HIDDEN VOICE ANTHOLOGY: VOLUME 1*
*VARIOUS AUTHORS*

*HIDDEN VOICE ANTHOLOGY: VOLUME 2*
*VARIOUS AUTHORS*

*TEN POEMS FOR PRIDE*
*SARAH PRITCHARD & JOEL SADLER*

*BOY(ISH) VEST*
*CARSON WOLFE*

Printed in Great Britain
by Amazon

11368106R00031